Are there no
communion?

Free of Man's fetters I dwell 'neath this mask of seeming.

A.M.

THE
GIFT OF
YOU

AN ANTHOLOGY OF LOVE & SORROW
AIDAN MARUS

SPECIAL THANKS TO

K.H. for your encouragement and providing me the spark for this literary work. And thanks to the forebears of our forebears for passing on to us their creative imaginings.

FOR K.H.

Who has conquered tribulation and emerged unbroken from the twisted blackness of the world. The most sacred thing within me bows before you with veneration.

You are mighty.

A.M.

DRAWINGS IN INK BY THE HAND OF

AIDAN MARUS

CONTENTS

AUTHOR'S NOTE

Do you not know? From black shadow this scarlet thing of flesh has come forth, its silent beating made sonorous; an imposing thunder where once all was silent.

Verily, I am awoken. And once more I feel a longing for life and an aching for love. For this I take to the pen, and for the urging of my heart I lay before you that which is hidden within me.

A.M.

The Gift of
You

The First
Time

When first I beheld

you, the world waxed silent forthwith, and no sound was known to me but the deep, booming thrum of my heart.

And my sight fell under a puissant spell, and would heed naught but your golden tresses and the nectar about your lips.

And for a fleeting beat of my heart, I felt a fear enfold me for I thought myself lost unto the world as I began to drift beyond

Creation into a silvery haze.

And when the argent sheen about me was no more, I found myself upon a soft, flaxen strand, and I beheld a golden horizon speckled with a thousand setting suns.

Then all was swept away, and consciousness retook me, and I returned to the world.

And I knew, then, that it

was *you* whom I had sought in the thousand dreams I had dreamt, and whom I had loved in the thousand lives I had lived.

And with febrile heart I went to you: a goddess made flesh, and we were joined.

And you set my heart afire, and it burned with a yearning and a longing so, that its flames eclipsed the mighty Sun in its heavenly perch.

But the way of the world cannot be stopped, and all things must pass...

And too soon you will depart me to pluck the stars from the heavens that you may spread their light upon the world.

While for your egress, a deep sadness hath cast its sable shadow upon me, and my joy and my sorrow are come together in a tussle and a dance about my laden heart.

And I am lost unto myself,
and a madness has become
the world.

The
Jacaranda
Tree

On the gloaming of

this day, I walked a walk upon dithering feet to lose the madness foist upon my grieving heart, when I chanced upon a jacaranda tree.

So I paused before its twisting roots, and I looked to its flower-bound limbs, and spake to it with a maddened fervor.

And within my laden words I evinced to it the pain and joy that encumbered my piteous heart.

And for my words, a shiver ran up the bole, and its leaves took to quivering, and it wept tears of purple-blue florets, and covered the ground in a blanket of velvet petals.

"Do you weep for my pain, tree?" I asked it.

"Nay," with a dejected voice it replied. "I weep for I have no heart, human.

"Would I could know but a fragment of the love you bear, and the aching of your laden heart bedsides.

"And fain I drink of your tears that art imbued with the sweetness of your sorrow and the evanescence of your joy."

And together we wept, wet and velvet tears entwined, before the eye of the setting sun.

The Gift

Many seasons had

passed, and many things and many thoughts had come to be and expired besides.

Yet our chance meet had brought forth from lost memory that thing that once was. Nay, not a lost memory, but a dream of a dream, and a thought of a thought, and an imagining of my heart.

Verily, I had thought my heart listless, and love was a quality lost and forgotten unto me; a thing of fables and imaginings. But with you my heart hath found communion, and for you it hath risen from its barrow[1] and found virility.

And never in all my moiling days and all my peace-giving nights, nor in the reveries of my awakening or in the wakefulness of my

[1] figurative; an ancient burial ground

slumber, had I known a greater gift than that of you.

For this my gratitude is without bound, and I am overcome with a hunger to repay you in kind.

Verily, for you I would enfold the constellations in a ribbon of scarlet silk, and make of them a supernal gift.

Or I would thieve the

gilded chariot of Helios[2],
and take you across the
empyrean abreast the
august Sun.

But for all this, fortune is
unkind, and the world
hath plotted to tear us
asunder. And for this cruel
fate my sorrow is deep,
and my pain is great.

Nay, the depth of my
sorrow and the greatness

[2] from Greek mythology: god of the Sun

of my pain are so, that my
heart hath wept away the
verve of my spirit, and
my eyes no longer care for
the hues and shapes of the
world, and I am a broken
thing.

I Dwell

My mind dwells

upon my heart, and my heart dwells upon you.

It is dayspring, and I am awoken, and my mind dwells upon my heart, and my heart dwells upon you.

It is noontide, and as I break the fast of morning 'neath the shade of a violet-flowered tree, my mind dwells upon my heart, and my heart dwells upon you.

It is eventide, and I relieve

my hunger with refection, and my thirst with red potation, and still my mind dwells upon my heart, and my heart dwells upon you.

And in my bedchamber I lay somnolent, and as my leaden eyes fasten, my mind dwells upon my heart, and my heart dwells upon you.

Nyx[3] has placed her sable
veil upon the world, and
I dream a mirthful dream,
and my dream dwells
upon a golden goddess,
and that goddess is you.

And many years have
passed uncounted– a mass
of memories beyond
recollection, and yet the
power of time cannot
extinguish the thought of
you. And as I lay in the

[3] from Greek mythology: the goddess of night.

bed of my looming death,
my mind dwells upon my
heart, and my heart dwells
upon you.

And now the heavens have
fallen upon the world, and
the   seas   swelled   and
seethed   and   were   made
into   mist,   and   from   the
earth's   bowels   spewed
great   fires   and   flowing
rock,   and   all   mankind
hath   drank   from   the

waters of Lethe[4], and forever has passed, and all has come to end.

And yet, in this white nothingness, my mind dwells upon my heart, and my heart dwells upon you.

[4] from Greek mythology: one of five rivers in Hades, where those who drank from it would experience absolute forgetfulness

Beholden

At noontide, as my

heart ached with longing, I drifted into a stupor, and found myself abreast my beloved in a dreamland of my mind's making, and we bound our lips, and made a wreath of our fingers.

And though our lips were loath to come apart, they left their wet embrace, and my beloved spoke to me with a lilting voice, and said, "Are there not others about you, dearest, whom would steal your heart whilst I am away?"

Said I, "My heart is in thrall to you, and beholden to no other. Verily, not the passing of all time nor the leagues of all space can wither this love for you I bear.

"And if you should fear these maidens about me, and if they should engender in you a whit of disquiet, then know that their maidenhood infects me with apathy and disdain, and I would with a terrible ire blame them for your lost peace, and loathe them all with fever and frenzy.

"Verily, I would not barter a thread of your tress for all the mountains gravid with riches, nor for all the lost treasures 'neath the stormy seas. Nay, not all the fortunes of Mankind bestrewn the heavens and earth could break this bond about my heart.

"And if the ancient Gods of Love should assay me with their beguiling songs and enchanted quivers, they would flee defeated, and suffer ignominy for their foundering[5].

"And I would sooner rive the moon from the heavens, and extinguish the flaming candles scattered about the welkin

[5] the gods of love would suffer public shame or disgrace for their failure, and would run away in defeat

in eventide than be parted from you.

"And fain I would dwell forevermore in the blackest pits of Tartarus[6], 'mongst demons and cursed angels, than bring a frown about your roseate lips.

"Verily, my heart doth prostrate itself before you,

[6] from Greek mythology: a dungeon below Hades where wicked souls are punished

and I am beholden."

The Arrant Lord

What is Love but

the arrant lord of Men?

She, like a frenzied tempest, at whim would lay waste the land, and with a touch soft as down and sweet as pain would build her grand temple in the deep recess of your sacred heart.

In her arms the fearsome beast would lay a suckling babe, and the quarry would become a mighty hunter.

She would with a breath
engender even the most
callus heart with humility
and brittle fettle.

She is wrathful and
unforgiving, and as gentle
as plume against your
yearning flesh.

She would with a whisper
make a fool the wise
scholar, and the quivering
coward a hero of lore.

Her lament would leave
in thy bosom a shattered

heart, and her merry song would lift you beyond the empyrean upon pinions of love.

We are her minions ever faithful, and by her throne doth even the great and mighty bow.

Said My Beloved

Said the child with a

smile to her mother, "Mother, how great is your love for me?"

And with a beaming grin, her mother stretched out her arms to their greatest breadth and said, "Greater than the reach of mine arms."

Said the little girl, "And no more, mother?"

Replied her mother amused, "Nay, and all the stars and sun-filled days therewithal."

And the little girl smiled a smile that could thaw the heart of the Grecian god of North Wind.

And then the little girl blossomed into a comely maiden, and enthralled the heart of a man.

And she asked her beloved, "How great is your love for me?"

And her beloved replied, "I

have not words for this
love I bear."

And the maiden frowned
a frown, and she said,
"Know you not our love?"

And for her frown, the
man's heart was shattered
and mended in a trice, and
then shattered once more,
and he said, "Nay, O
keeper of my heart. Verily,
there is naught liken to
my love for you; not in
all the lore of the Gods,
nor in all the legends of

Man.

"And if I would fashion a thread of this love, I could weave Creation anew, and the void beyond withal.

"Verily, not with all things living and unliving bound to this earth, nor with all the great bodies floating about the firmament, could you fill the yawning depth that is my love for you."

Paragon of Beauty

"Beauty is the

crape myrtle in summer bloom, and the verdant blades dancing about its thirsty feet," said Demeter[7].

"Nay," said I, "Beauty is my beloved."

"Beauty is the morning wind in a caper about a white billow," said Aura[8].

"Nay," said I, "Beauty is my

[7] from Greek mythology: the goddess of the harvest

[8] from Greek mythology: the goddess (Titaness) of the breeze and cool morning wind. Here Aura describes beauty as a morning breeze dancing around a white cloud

beloved."

"Beauty is the full bloom of the silver Moon, and its circlet of lambent light that breaks the night," said Selena[9].

"Nay," said I, "Beauty is my beloved."

"Beauty is the great burning sphere beyond the ether, and a terrible

[9] from Greek mythology: goddess of the moon

wreathe of coiling flame sprouting from an ocean of fire," said Helios[10].

"Nay," said I, "Beauty is my beloved."

"Beauty is the peace-giving murmur of a rill, and the crystalline ripplets of a mountain fount," said Tethys[11].

[10] from Greek mythology: here Helios, the sun-god, describes beauty as the sun, and the flames that erupt from its surface
[11] from greek mythology: goddess of the sea

"Nay," said I, "Beauty is my beloved."

"Beauty is a vermilion fleck about the offing at dayspring," said Eos[12].

"Nay," said I, "Beauty is my beloved."

"Beauty is the moribund star descending upon bright wings of flame from the heavens," said

[12] from Greek mythology: goddess of the dawn. Here Eos describes beauty as a red streak on the sea's horizon during sunrise

Asteria[13].

"Nay," said I, "Beauty is my beloved."

And then my beloved came forth, and they were all smote with awe; and they wept for her beauty and the aching of their hearts, and in unison spoke and said, "Aye,

---

[13] from Greek mythology: the goddess of falling stars. Here Asteria describes beauty as a dying star flying down from the heavens upon wings made of fire

beauty is your beloved."

Sanguine

The world is not

blackening; tis only the mantle of eventide that brings forth the argent Mother of Tides, and would scatter about the heavens a mottle of glistering light.

The wilted willow is not weeping; tis only its serrate leaves longing to taste the life-giving soil about its twisting roots, and to kiss the many green blades bestrewn the earth.

The horizon is not bleeding; tis only the vermilion lips of the Sun brushing against the Earth to wake it from its slumber, and an avowal of love to the beasts and verdure whom art enervate in the night.

I am not broken for the egress of my beloved; tis only the longing and yearning of my heart that doth paint a stain of sorrow on the mask of joy I wear.

And yet, mayhap I speak false, for my beating heart defies me, and this leaden mask of joy grows weary as I descend into a tenebrous void toward the cradle of my mourning.

Bond of
Amity

To whom a gratitude

is owed, whom hath made gentle a hardened man, why do you depart me? I ask it only once, yet it echoes forevermore in the deep recess of my mind.

Nay, do not answer, for your reason is known to me, and I fear my words art despairing and reckless.

You had come to me with a grieving heart, and for your pain I was filled with sorrow. So I took you into mine arms, and swept

away your tears with these
written words and a
whisper-song of my
splayed heart.

And heedless we danced a
wild dance, and reveled in
our joy & sorrow, and
kept hidden the whispers
of our hearts, and all was
fraught with peril.

But I evince to you now
that this thing we had is
no more, and its memory
sullied and has become a
shell.

Nay, you need not fret,
and do not think to weep,
for this shell is in fact a
seed sowed 'neath the skin
of my heart; and this seed
hath sprouted into a bond
of amity; and this bond
shall break the fetters of
time and pay no regard to
the sundering leagues of
the world.

A Letter to You

To *sh*e, whom hath

engaged my heart,

Fret not, you are made whole, and the Universe smiles upon you.

Verily, let the tribulations of Life rage and crash against you; but it is for naught, for you are a rock that cannot be withered; that cannot be broken.

And let evil come; but it is folly, for you are more potent than ever it shall be; verily, you are a piercing light in the darkness of the world.

And let chaos and hardship dance about you; but they canst not sway you, for you are unwavering and determined in those things you have examined with sedulity.

And if ever there shall be a needing in your tender heart, you needs only give voice, and stalwart I will come.

Soliloquy

Come to me with

your grieving heart.

Let me heal the deep
wound that steals away
the peace of your nights.

Let me put to sleep the
gnawing sorrow that
dwells unseen within you,
but that only I can see.

Let me mend the crazing
rift about your weeping
heart with the limpid sap
of my soul and a soothing
susurrus from my lips.

With untainted love and
the blood of my febrile
heart I will lead you to
peace and sow within you
the seed of love anew.

Find in the temple of my
spirit solace and refuge
that you may freely brood
and gnash and tear at your
bosom, and then restore
yourself and rest 'neath its
tranquil white dome ever
cast in twilight.

Let me take your pain and
your sadness and make

them my own that you
may regard the beauty of
the heavens once again,
and fill the world with the
sound of your laughter.

Then, when the wings of
your gentle heart are
whole again depart me,
and take with you a
fragment of my being.

Verily, only fragments of
me remain.

And as I drift upon the sea
of your sorrow haunted by

your waning memory, my
mind dwells upon a fate I
cannot escape: that for all
my days I will remain
alone— a healer to the
grieving and a lover to
the broken hearted.

Denouement

Do not think I am

without sorrow. Verily, I am withered and forlorn, and a broken thing.

Nay, not I alone, but the whole of the world is broken besides.

Even the mountain hath lost its height, and canst no longer taste the kiss of a passing billow.

And even the sea hath lost its depth, and become a wan and hollow thing.

And the blazing Sun is afire no more, and its flames art black and withered.

And the argent sphere about the heavens hath lost its sheen and become a dreary rock; and even the stars about it have resolved to hide behind a veil of darkness.

And the welkin hath forgotten the day and the touch of playful pinions, and now dwells alone in black shadow.

And all about me is dark
and silent and dead.

And yet, these crimson
rivulets race madly about
the many burrows of flesh
bestrewn my body.

And though my heart
wanes, its pulse is a wild
keen, and for this keening
I am overcome and given
to madness.

Fain I would rive this red,

beating thing from its ivory cage to put to an end, and silence its wailing thrum that without pity subdues the song of the sea and the wind.

Verily, *all is madness.*

And the season of merriment and blossoming is now sorrow and decay;

And the vast mantle woven of blue æther canst

no longer carry the Sun;

And my lungs drink of the air, but the air is a miasma;

And all that was splendor and song is now an emptiness and a lament.

Cursed heart, thou art rent, and thine tears art a fetid red ichor[14] that doth becloud my sight.

[14] bloodlike fluid

Be still...

...now a lambent light
becomes my sight, and
from this very dark dream
I am awoken.

And my wit hath returned
to me, and my faculties
are restored, and I am
once more lachrymose
with joy for the wondrous
fettle of the world and its
great beauty.

And the white crest of the
mountain doth rise

beyond the ether, and doth bathe in an ocean of speckled light.

And the sea doth brim with life, and doth sway for the sweet lilt of a Merrow-maiden's[15] song, and too doth rejoice for the ligneous touch of the seafarer's barque.

And the life-giving Sun doth burn bright with fervor and doth slay the

[15] a mermaid

shadows of the world with splendent blades of fire.

And the glimmering Moon doth dance a jig about the firmament and doth make a bond of love with star and sea.

And the welkin is aglow with a weave of gold and cerulean light, and doth lift the wings of sparrows upon the winds of heaven.

And all about me is laughter and song and

golden light.

Verily, the red tears of my splayed heart are in truth a soothing nectar that will mend your wounds and efface the pains of your heart;

And the skins of our hearts will be branded with the fire of our memories, and we will forever be joined in an eternal bond, hollowed and unyielding.

And mayhap in this life or another, we may yet come together, and once more we will make a wreath of our hands and a bond of our lips and a dance of our hearts. And we will walk abreast unchallenged, and the bond of our love will make a mockery of eternity and endure the death of time.

For this I can only dream.

For this I can only hope.

Do not forget me.

Thank you for reading. This work is dear to my heart, and not without courage do I expose my naked thoughts to you. I had originally begun writing as a hobby, purely for

100

personal fulfillment, and to satisfy an innate urge for self-expression. Truly, I had not originally intended these works for the public. Only after persistent prodding by friends did I decide to publish my writings. But one person, in particular, who touched my life in a special way, had provided the motivation to put forth such a sensitive composition.

The works in this book were inspired by true events, and by my childhood notions on the nature of love. For me, however, real world experiences have been far removed from the romantic imaginings of my childhood. People are too busy in this modern life, too occupied with self-entertainment, too broken, too wanting, too married to expectations, and often marred by their own experiences. Nevertheless, the notion of true love is not dead to me, and never will be. Truly, there are many of us who are lucky enough to experience it, and there is no greater bond in the whole of our existence.

Thank you, again, for joining me in this literary representation of love and heartbreak. If you have questions, or feedback, or want to explore some part of this book in more depth, please feel free to communicate with me by email at marus.aidan@gmail.com.

Yours,
Aidan Marus